w.slough.gov.uk

ug

# GEETA'S DAY

Slough Libraries

38 0674 1250 1782

| SLOUGH LIBRARY & INFORMATION | |
| --- | --- |
| 501782 | |
| CH915.4 | 16-Dec-05 |
| PETERS | |
| | |

*For the people of Orissa*
To Amrita, Prita, and Kunu for their inspiration,
and to Janetta, Yvonne, and Sophie for making it happen

*Geeta's Day* copyright © Frances Lincoln Limited 1999
Text and illustrations copyright © Prodeepta Das 1999

First published in Great Britain in 1999 by Frances Lincoln Limited,
4 Torriano Mews, Torriano Avenue, London NW5 2RZ
First paperback edition 2002

All rights reserved

No part of this publication may be reproduced, stored in a retrieval system,
or transmitted, in any form, or by any means, electrical, mechanical, photocopying,
recording or otherwise without the prior written permission of the publisher or a licence
permitting restricted copying. In the United Kingdom such licences are issued by
the Copyright Licensing Agency, 90 Tottenham Court Road, London W1P 9HE.

British Library Cataloguing in Publication Data available on request

ISBN 0-7112-2024-7

Designed by Sophie Pelham

Set in Hiroshige Book and Caslon Regular.

Printed in China

3 5 7 9 8 6 4

# GEETA'S DAY

## From Dawn to Dusk in an Indian Village

## Prodeepta Das

FRANCES LINCOLN

# AUTHOR'S NOTE

India is a country of villages. Some people are born, grow up and die in their village without ever moving to another place.

The village is one great family. Everyone knows everybody else. Children roam freely and use the whole village as their playground. Small children are so spoilt by their grandparents and older children that they spend very little time with their own mothers. In the village, older people are never called by their first names: they are known as "brother", "sister", "uncle" or "auntie".

The village I have chosen to photograph is in the state of Orissa, in eastern India. But the events of Geeta's day could be happening in almost any plains village in India.

*Prodeepta*

INDIA

*Orissa*

Geeta is six years old.

She lives in Janla, a small village like any other Indian village, sharing a home with her parents, her three brothers Sidhartha, Abhay and Raj, and her sister Rekha. Her two uncles live next door with their families. Geeta's grandmother lives there too. Geeta's father, Bidyadhar Sahu, is head teacher at the village school.

Morning in Janla begins at dawn, just before the sun rises. Geeta wakes up and watches her *aai* (grandmother) do her morning *puja* (worship), hands folded before her face and lips moving as she says her prayer. Geeta's family are Hindus, and puja is an important part of their religion.

*Puja Most houses have two shrines, one indoors and one outside. The outdoor shrine is an earthen mound with a basil plant growing on top. People offer prayers there in the morning and evening.*

Then the children rush into the courtyard to brush their teeth and take a bucket bath. Geeta likes to brush her teeth with a special twig taken from the nearby *neem* tree.

*NEEM is famous for its medicinal powers. It is used in toothpaste to keep gums healthy. The bark is boiled and mixed with turmeric to cure skin diseases, and the leaves are used to reduce malarial fever. Chicken-pox sufferers find relief from their itchy skin by sleeping on a bed of neem leaves.*

After their bucket bath, the children help their mother with the morning's cooking. Geeta's father is giving extra coaching to some other children, so Geeta and her brothers and sister join in too.

An hour later, *jalakhia* (big breakfast) is ready.

JALAKHIA *Sometimes Geeta's big breakfast is rice, dal or lentil and mashed aubergine or fried vegetables, sometimes puffed rice with yogurt, sugar and banana.*

By 10 o'clock it is already feeling hot and sticky, and it is time to walk to school. On her way, Geeta passes some local tradesmen.

The *kamar* (blacksmith) is hard at work making tools.

 The *bhandari* (barber) is shaving a customer in his shop.

The *bania* (goldsmith) is busy shaping gold and silver jewellery.

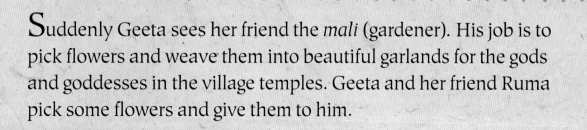

Suddenly Geeta sees her friend the *mali* (gardener). His job is to pick flowers and weave them into beautiful garlands for the gods and goddesses in the village temples. Geeta and her friend Ruma pick some flowers and give them to him.

The school day begins with a prayer. The children fold their hands together and sing, "Oh kind Lord, teach me to be good. I need neither wealth nor help from other people."

This morning, Geeta is learning arithmetic. In a small classroom, 40 children sit shoulder to shoulder. Those who have not done their homework hide in the back row, hoping to escape the teacher's eye!

At last they break for games. Geeta's class divides into two teams, and they make a line of flip-flop sandals to separate the teams to play *ha do do*. You have to run really fast to win! Another game they often play is *chaka chaka bhaunri*. But Geeta's favourite game is *puchi*.

Ha do do *A member of one team goes over to the other side, chanting "ha do do", and tries to touch the other team and run back to her own side. The other team tries to hold her down.*

Chaka chaka bhaunri *While her teacher sings "Turning around in a wheel...", Geeta holds hands with the other girls and they go round and round until their heads spin!*

Puchi *The girls squat on the ground and shuffle around, twisting their feet. The one who doesn't fall over, wins.*

9

At lunch time, Geeta and her friends share out the pickles and relishes they have brought with them. Free school meals were started recently to encourage children from poorer families to come to school.

After lunch there are more lessons. Today they are reading about the Car Festival of Puri.

*Puri is an important Hindu holy place, where the god Jagannath is brought out every year in a huge colourful chariot. Thousands gather to see him. The word 'juggernaut' comes from his name.*

Once school is over for the day Geeta sets off for home.

Geeta gets home to find a vendor showing his wares. Vendors travel from village to village on foot or by bicycle, each offering something different.

Some sell costume jewellery, bangles, *tippis*, or *kajal*. Some sell *saris*. Others sell fresh or dried fish.

TIPPIS *are the coloured dots women and girls wear on their foreheads.*
KAJAL *Women put this black paste on their eyelids to make their eyes look large.*
SARIS *These are lengths of colourful material which Indian women wear as dresses.*

Geeta thinks the nicest vendors are the ones who sell toys, sweets and ice-cream!

At holiday time, Geeta likes to swim in the village pond. Some of her friends show off, diving and making a splash. The pond is used not only for bathing, but for washing clothes and watering the fields nearby. Geeta's village has a number of tube wells sunk deep in the ground, which pump up safe water for drinking and cooking.

In the monsoon months from June, to September, it rains a lot, and the village *danda* (street) turns into a fast-flowing stream. Geeta always gets excited when this happens. She folds pieces of old newspaper into paper boats, and jumps for joy when her boat floats past her friend's boat, which has got stuck on a pebble.

In May and June it gets very hot and most people rest during the afternoon. Geeta and her sister wait until their parents and aai are fast asleep, then slip quietly out. It is much more fun playing see-saw on the bullock cart!

The mango grove is another tempting place, especially during the Raja Festival. Today the children go there to play on the *doli* - a homemade rope swing with a sack for a seat. Geeta is thrilled when Ruma pushes her hard, and her stretched-out feet nearly touch the high branches of the mango tree.

*RAJA FESTIVAL. During the festival, held in May, when the grove is full of ripening mangoes, village girls come out in colourful new dresses to play on the swings and sing the latest hit songs from films.*

As the day slowly cools down, the women come out on to their verandas to sew and chat. Some of the men play *pasa*, a kind of chess game. Geeta and her friends watch while the men shout and throw their dice, hoping to get a winner.

Sometimes the travelling holy man arrives, carrying the goddess Mangala on his head and beating his gong. When Geeta gives him some food or money, he blesses her by striking her head gently with his stick, and moves on to the next house.

Dusk falls. As the sun disappears, the village elders gather in the temple courtyard for a *nishap*. Whatever the villagers discuss, the *mukhia* (the oldest person, and head of the village), always has the final word.

*MANGALA. The goddess Mangala protects the village against ill fortune, such as natural disasters and diseases, and a blessing from her ensures that new ventures are successful. NISHAP is a meeting of villagers held to sort out local disputes.*

After an hour's study, Geeta joins her family for their evening meal. They all cluster around to share a big plateful of food. There is always rice, *dal* (lentils) and fried or curried vegetables, with fish once a week and occasionally meat.

This evening there is something extra-special for dinner. Geeta's friend's granny has brought over a big handful of pumpkin flowers picked early that morning. Fried in batter, they're delicious, a speciality of the rainy season. And there's another favourite of Geeta's: *pith*a, a fried mixture of white lentils ground with rice powder.

After dinner aai tells the children a story from the *Ramayana*. Then they hang up their mosquito net.

When the children are tucked in to bed, Geeta's parents bring out the *Bhagavadgita* (holy book) from the household shrine, and the neighbors listen to her father reading from its sacred verses.

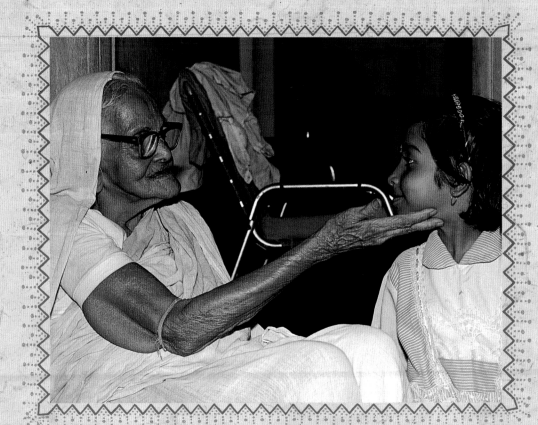

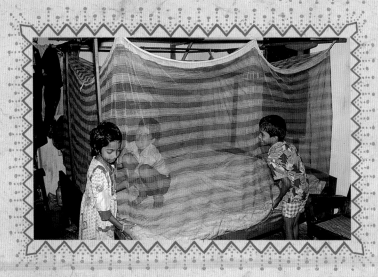

*THE RAMAYANA and the Mahabharata are India's two great religious epics. The Ramayana tells the story of Prince Rama and his banishment into the forest for 14 years. It is a story of good triumphing over evil.*

*THE BHAGAVADGITA forms part of the Mahabharata. It describes Lord Krishna, the Hindu god who embodies virtue, and teaches how to lead a virtuous life.*

Geeta falls asleep to
the distant sounds of
drums, harmonium and
cymbals in the temple
courtyard, where people
have gathered for an
evening of singing.
   Sleep well, Geeta!

# MORE ABOUT INDIA

## INDIA, THE PAST

India has a long and rich history. Just like a magnet, it has attracted many visitors. Some have come to explore India's many wonders; others have come to rule the country and make money from its spices and jewels. The most recent foreign power to rule India was Great Britain (the British controlled India for about two hundred years).

India finally became independent in 1947, when a great Indian leader named Mahatma Gandhi led the people to freedom. At about the same time, part of India broke away to become a separate country called Pakistan. Later, the eastern part of Pakistan broke away again and became a separate country called Bangladesh.

India has made great progress since independence. Now it is among the world's top industrialised countries.

## INDIA, THE LAND

India is the seventh largest country in the world, and almost a billion people live there. It is the home of the tallest mountains in the world – the Himalayas – and the great Ganges, a river that Indian people believe to be sacred. India also has long, beautiful coastlines and large areas of rainforest, where wild animals such as lions, tigers and elephants live and thousands of exotic birds fill the air with their songs.

## RELIGION IN INDIA

India is the birthplace of four religions: Hinduism, Buddhism, Jainism and Sikhism. Most Indian people are Hindus, but there are also many Muslims and Christians.

Hindu society was originally organised around the caste system, although this is beginning to be less important. The caste system was developed hundreds of years ago and divides people into four castes, or groups, according to what type of work they do: the first caste are *Brahmins*, or priests; the second are *Kshatriyas*, warriors; the third are *Vaishyas*, business people and traders; and the fourth are *Sudras*, who do the laundry for the other three castes and serve as barbers, blacksmiths and labourers. People who weren't any of these were called untouchables and were given the worst jobs. Mahatma Gandhi saw how unfair this system was and renamed the untouchables the *harijans*, which means "God's people."

## PEOPLE IN INDIA

The most important part of Indian society is the family, which, in addition to children and their parents, also includes uncles and aunts, cousins, and grand-parents and great-grandparents. Indian people see themselves as part of a wider family first and as individuals second, and they are bound up in a network of care and affection. Most young people marry the person their parents and elders choose. This is called an "arranged marriage". Indian people are very friendly: guests always receive special treatment, and people go out of their way to make visitors from other countries feel at home.

Going to the cinema is a favourite pastime in India. To be popular, an Indian film must have plenty of songs and dances. The Indian film industry is so big that the city of Bombay (called *Mumbai* in India) makes more films each year than Hollywood and has been nicknamed Bollywood.

# LANGUAGE IN INDIA

India is a vast country, and each region has its own language. Many of these Indian languages now share some of the same words because people have moved from one part of India to another and taken their languages with them. Indian films, which mostly use the Indian languages Hindi, Urdu, Telugu, Tamil and Bengali, have also brought Indian languages together. And because India was ruled by other countries in the past, foreign languages – such as Portuguese, English, and French – have brought about changes in Indian language too. In much the same way, many Indian words have found their way into English – for example, bungalow, bazaar, dungarees, curry and pyjamas.

The national language of India is Hindi, but people who live in southern India think this is unfair because Hindi isn't usually spoken in this area. Having so many languages in one country can get very complicated! To try to make things easier, Indian money is printed in all the major languages, including English and the names of many railway stations are written in English, the local language, and Hindi. In fact, if you went travelling around India, English would probably be the best language you could speak, as almost everyone would be able to understand you.

SOME HINDI WORDS AND PHRASES
namaste! (na-ma-stay) – hello!
phir milenge (feer mee-leng-ee) – goodbye
dhanyabad (dan-yah-bad) – thank you
kripaya (cri-pa-yah) – please
Meri nam Geeta hai. (merry nam Gee-ta hi) – My name is Geeta.
Ye meri ghar hai. (Ye merry gar hi) – This is my house.

# THE INDIAN WORDS IN THE BOOK

*aai* – grandmother

*bania* – goldsmith

Bengali – the language spoken in Bangladesh, and also in part of India

*Bhagavadgita* – a sacred Hindu text

*bhandari* – barber

*Brahmins* – the priests in the Hindu caste system

*chaka chaka bhaunri* – a playground game

*dal* – lentils

*danda* – street

*doli* – rope swing

Ganges – a great and holy Indian river

*ha do do* – a playground game

*harijans* – "God's people." This is how Mahatma Gandhi once described all the Indian people who didn't belong to any of the four Hindu castes.

Himalayas – the mountains in the north of India

Hindi – India's national language

Jagannath – a Hindu god who is worshipped at the festival of Puri

*jalakhia* – breakfast

Janla – Geeta's village

*kajal* – eye makeup

*kamar* – blacksmith

Krishna – the Hindu god of virtue

*Kshatriyas* – the warriors, the second Hindu caste

*Mahabharata* – a sacred Hindu text

Mahatma Gandhi – a famous Indian leader

*mali* – gardener

Mangala – the Hindu goddess of safe journeys

*mukhia* – the name for the head of a village

Mumbai – the Hindi name for Bombay, a city in western India

*neem* – a large Indian tree with many medicinal uses

*nishap* – a village meeting

Orissa – a state in eastern India

*pasa* – a game similar to chess

*pitha* – a pancake made out of beans and rice powder

*puja* – worship

*puchi* – a playground game

Puri – a holy place in India

Raja festival – an Indian festival held in May

*Rama* – the hero of the Ramayana story

*Ramayana* – a sacred Hindu text

*saris* – the dresses worn by Indian women

*Sudras* – the working people, the fourth Hindu caste

Tamil – an Indian language spoken in southern India

Telugu – an Indian language spoken in south-east India

*tippis* – the coloured dots Hindu women wear on their foreheads

Urdu – the language spoken in Pakistan and in parts of India

*Vaishyas* – the traders, the third Hindu caste

# INDEX